A Look At...

Insects and Spiders

WORLD
BOOK

a Scott Fetzer company
Chicago
www.worldbookonline.com

Staff:

Executive Committee

President
Donald D. Keller

Vice President and Editor
in Chief
Paul A. Kobasa

Vice President, Marketing/
Digital Products
Sean Klunder

Vice President,
International
Richard Flower

Director, Human Resources
Bev Ecker

Editorial

Associate Director,
Supplementary Publications
Scott Thomas

Associate Manager,
Supplementary Publications
Cassie Mayer

Researcher,
Supplementary Publications
Annie Brodsky

Manager, Indexing Services
David Pofelski

Manager, Contracts & Compliance
(Rights & Permissions)
Loranne K. Shields

Editorial Administration

Director, Systems and Projects
Tony Tills

Senior Manager, Publishing
Operations
Timothy Falk

Associate Manager,
Publishing Operations
Audrey Casey

Graphics and Design

Manager
Tom Evans

Manager, Cartographic Services
Wayne K. Pichler

Senior Cartographer
John Rejba

Book Design by
Matt Carrington

Senior Designer
Isaiah Sheppard

Contributing Designer
Lucy Lesiak

Photo Editor
Kathy Creech

Contributing Photo Editor
Clover Morell

Production

Director, Manufacturing and Pre-Press
Carma Fazio

Manufacturing Manager
Steven K. Hueppchen

Production/
Technology Manager
Anne Fritzinger

Proofreader
Emilie Schrage

World Book, Inc.
233 N. Michigan Avenue
Chicago, IL 60601

For information about other World Book publications,
visit our website at http://www.worldbookonline.com or
call **1-800-WORLDBK (967-5325).**
For information about sales to schools and libraries, call
1-800-975-3250 (United States), or **1-800-837-5365
(Canada).**

Library of Congress Cataloging-in-Publication Data
Insects and spiders
    p. cm. -- (A look at ...)
    Includes index.
    Summary: "An introduction to insects and spiders,
including their varieties, development, physical features,
behavior, and social organization. Features include fact
boxes, photographs, illustrations, a glossary, and a list
of recommended books and websites"—Provided by
publisher.
    ISBN 978-0-7166-1789-1
    1. Insects--Juvenile literature. 2. Spiders--Juvenile
literature. I. World Book, Inc.
QL467.2.I586 2011
595.7--dc22
                    2011006433

A Look At ...
Set ISBN 978-0-7166-1786-0

Printed in China by Shenzhen Donnelley Printing Co., Ltd.
Guangdong Province
1st printing July 2011

Picture Acknowledgments:

The publishers gratefully acknowledge the following sources for
photography. All illustrations and maps were prepared by WORLD
BOOK unless otherwise noted.

Front cover: Shutterstock

blickwinkel/Alamy Images 17; David Cole, Alamy Images 58; Custom
Life Science Images/Alamy Images 30; Scott Camazine,
Phototake/Alamy Images 34; Heather Angel, Natural Visions/Alamy
Images 40; Wildlife GmbH/Alamy Images 10; Breck Kent, Animals
Animals 36; Center for Disease Control and Prevention 45; Danny
Lehman, Corbis 42; Dreamstime 14, 16, 18, 26, 32, 33, 53, 54; Ian
Waldie, Getty Images 57; Mark Gibson, Index Stock 51; iStockphoto
36, 46; Pierre Holtz, Reuters/Landov 60; Matthias Schrader, Landov 56;
Bob Anderson, Masterfile 13; DK & Dennie Cody, Masterfile 31; Minden
Pictures/Masterfile 6, 8, 9, 11, 14, 22, 23, 24, 26, 27, 29, 41, 42, 52,
54; Robert Harding Images/Masterfile 28; Visuals Unlimited/Masterfile
47; Jeremy Woodhouse, Masterfile 49; Satoshi Kuribayashi, Minden
Pictures 34; Albert Lleal, Minden Pictures 35; Ingo Arndt, Nature Picture
Library 38; Stephen Dalton, Nature Picture Library 52; Scott Camazine,
Photo Researchers 24; Hans Pfletschinger, Peter Arnold
Inc./photolibrary 51; Johann Schumacher, Peter Arnold Inc./photolibrary
30; Shutterstock 5, 8, 10, 11, 12, 14, 18, 25, 28, 31, 38, 39, 41, 44,
47, 48, 50, 53, 58, 59, 60; Age fotostock/Superstock 4;
Exactostock/SuperStock 14, 15; imagebroker/SuperStock 17, 37, 44;
IndexStock/SuperStock 56; George Oze, SuperStock 20; Robert Harding
Images/SuperStock 43; Science Faction/Superstock 5; James Urbach,
SuperStock 21, 38; Gerry Bishop, Visuals Unlimited 55; Cheryl Hogue,
Visuals Unlimited 37; Gary Meszaros, Visuals Unlimited 55.

CONTENTS

There is a glossary on page 62. Terms defined in the glossary are in type
that looks like this on their first appearance on any spread (two facing pages).

Introducing Insects and Spiders

They scuttle across the floor. They hide under rocks. They buzz around the picnic basket. They're insects.

Insects live almost everywhere. You might not always see them because they are so small. But there are lots of them around. In fact, more of these creepy-crawly creatures live in our world than any other kind of animal!

What is an insect?

An insect is a small animal with six legs. Lots of other animals we think of as bugs are not insects. A worm is not an insect. Neither is a slug or a scorpion.

Is a spider an insect?

A spider is a different kind of animal altogether. A spider has eight legs, not six. Its body is a different shape, too. Many spiders live by hunting insects. So where there are insects, you will find spiders.

Arthropods all

All insects and spiders belong to the large group of animals called arthropods *(AHR thruh pods).* The word *arthropod* comes from two Greek words meaning "jointed feet." Actually, an insect's legs—not its feet—are jointed. All arthropods have jointed legs. Insects make up the largest class of arthropods. Examples of other animals in this group include crustaceans (lobsters and shrimp, among other animals), centipedes, scorpions, millipedes, daddy longlegs, and ticks.

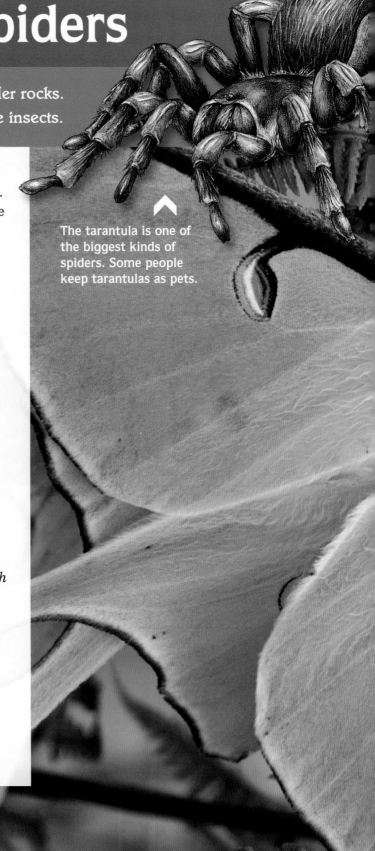

The tarantula is one of the biggest kinds of spiders. Some people keep tarantulas as pets.

Did You Know?

Scientists have named more than 1 ½ million kinds of animals. Of these, about 1 million are insects. Thousands of new kinds of insects are discovered every year. Scientists believe there may be from 5 million to 30 million kinds of insects still undiscovered!

The honey bee feeds on a juice made by flowers. Without insects, Earth would not have so many flowering plants.

Such insects as the luna moth have markings and coloration that help them to blend in with their surroundings.

Insects everywhere

Insects come in all shapes and sizes. Some insects are beautiful. Some look scary. Some scurry across the ground, some fly, and some **burrow** (dig a hole) into the ground. Insects have many ways of finding food, making homes, and escaping from **predators** (hunting animals).

The rhinoceros beetle is named for the horn on its head. There are hundreds of thousands of different kinds of beetles.

Features of Insects

The world of insects includes some of the most beautiful and fantastic animals on Earth. Insects show a stunning variety in size, color, and form.

Insect bodies

An insect's body has three main parts: the head, **thorax** (middle), and **abdomen.** Most insects also have a pair of **antennae** (feelers), and many have wings. An insect breathes air through holes along the sides of its body.

An insect has a skeleton on the outside of its body, called the exoskeleton. The exoskeleton is made of material lighter and stronger than bone. It protects an insect like a suit of armor.

Insects have one pair of legs connected to each segment of the thorax. Each leg has five main segments, with movable joints between the segments. When humans walk, we balance ourselves on one leg as we step forward with the other. When insects walk, they usually move the middle leg on one side at the same time that they move the front and hind legs on the other. In this way, they are always firmly supported, like a three-legged stool.

An insect's head includes mouthparts, eyes, and antennae. Insects have mouths adapted either for chewing or sucking.

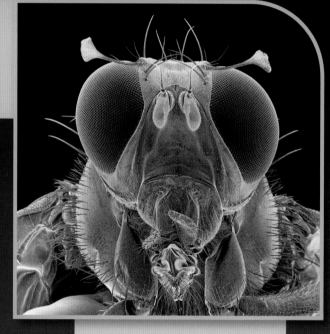

A magnified image of a fruit fly shows the insect's huge eyes, as well as hairs and spines on its body that serve as touch organs.

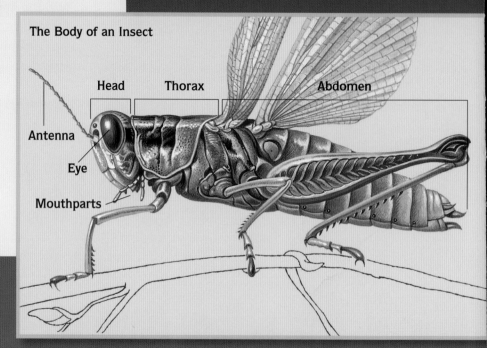

The Body of an Insect

Antenna
Eye
Mouthparts
Head
Thorax
Abdomen

Moths use their feathery antennae chiefly to smell. Male moths can smell the scent of female moths from as far as 5 miles (8 kilometers) away.

Seeing and smelling

Most adult insects have two enormous compound eyes. Compound eyes are made up of separate lenses—the eyes of some insects have thousands. Light gathered by all the lenses combines to form a complete picture. Many insects with compound eyes can see well, but only over short distances.

Almost all insects have two antennae. They use their antennae chiefly to smell and to feel. Many insects also use their antennae to hear, and some use them to taste. Many insects become helpless if their antennae are removed.

Insects Are Tough

Insects are small but amazingly tough. Many have enormous strength for their size. Humans have fewer than 700 muscles, but a tiny caterpillar may have as many as 4,000 muscles! Insects can easily lift more than their own weight. They could out-sprint and out-jump an Olympic athlete!

Many insects can also live in water as cold as ice. Some insects can come back to life after being frozen solid!

Ants are insects that live almost everywhere on land. The only places you will not find ants are the bitterly cold polar regions.

Some ants live in underground tunnels. Some build earth mounds. Others live inside trees or in hollow parts of plants. There are ants that build their nests from the leaves of trees. And there are some, like the army ants, that spend their lives on the move.

The body of an ant

Like all insects, an ant has a body with three parts. The head has two eyes, two **antennae,** and two jawlike structures called mandibles. The **thorax** has six legs. In the **abdomen** at the rear are the organs used to digest food and reproduce. Some ants also have a stinger.

The ant colony

Ants are known as **social insects** because they live in organized communities. Ants are not the only social animals in the insect world. Termites and some kinds of bees and wasps also live in communities. A community of animals is called a **colony.**

Some ant colonies are small, with as few as a dozen ants living in each one. Others have hundreds, thousands, or even millions of ants.

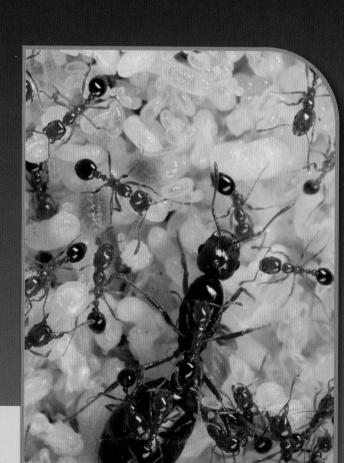

Ants look similar to termites, but they have narrow waists and bent antennae.

The queen and worker ants among pupae (developing ants in cocoons). The queen is much larger than other ants in the colony.

The queen and her subjects

The head of the ant colony is the queen, a special female ant. The queen's main job is to lay eggs. Most other members of the colony are worker ants. They are females, but they do not lay eggs. Their job is to build the nest, search for food, care for the young, and fight **predators.** A few male ants live in the nest at certain times. Their only job is to mate with young queens, who will then start new colonies. Soon after mating, the male ants die.

Super ants

Ants are astonishingly strong. An ant can lift an object 10 times as heavy as itself. The strongest human weight-lifters can lift about three times their own body weight. Some ants can lift objects 50 times as heavy as themselves. Imagine a person lifting a full-grown elephant! That's how strong these super ants are.

The bulldog ant of Australia grabs a passing honey bee. These fierce hunters are known for their excellent vision and tremendous speed.

Big and Small

Ants come in many different sizes. A dwarf ant named *Strumigenys* grows to less than 0.04 inch (0.1 centimeter) long. One of the largest ants is the *Dinoponera grandis*, or giant hunting ant. It can reach more than 1.5 inches (4 centimeters) long.

Of all the insects, ants have some of the most amazing ways of finding and storing food. Some ants are harvesters, farmers, or living honeypots.

Harvesters

Harvester ants collect seeds and store them in special chambers inside their nests. In doing so, they always have a supply of food in case food outside the nest becomes scarce. They tear off the tough husks of the seeds and chew the kernels (insides) into a soft pulp called ant bread. Then they squeeze out the liquid and swallow it. They feed this paste to one another and to their young.

"Dairy" farmers

Other ants are "dairy" farmers. They live mainly on a sugary liquid called honeydew. They get the honeydew from other insects, mostly from aphids and other plant lice. Plant lice suck juices from plants. The juices contain more sugar and water than the lice need, so they get rid of the excess as honeydew. Dairying ants visit the plants on which aphids feed. When an ant strokes an aphid with its **antennae,** the aphid releases a drop of honeydew, and the ant licks it up.

Dairy-farmer ants take care of their "herds." They protect the aphids and drive off other insects. Some ants carry their plant lice into the warmth of the ant nest in winter. Others keep herds of plant lice on roots inside the ant nest. When a young queen ant leaves the nest to start a new ant **colony,** she carries an egg-laying plant louse with her to start a new dairy herd.

When dairy farmer ants stroke aphids with their antennae, the aphids release drops of honeydew. The ants eat the sugary liquid.

Leaf-cutter ants use leaves and other plant materials to grow gardens of fungi inside their nest. They use fungi as a food source.

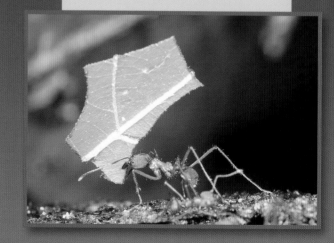

Ants work together to perform many tasks. These worker ants form a living bridge to travel from leaf to leaf.

Partners

Some kinds of ants have a special relationship with certain kinds of plants. Some ants are attracted to a kind of plant by a special food that the plant grows for the ants to eat. In return for a home and food, the ants protect the plant. They drive off leaf-eating insects. They will even sting sheep, deer, or elephants that try to eat the leaves of their plant. Scientists call this kind of partnership symbiosis. Both partners—the plant and the ants—benefit from the arrangement.

Honeypot ants are living storage tanks that hang from the roof, waiting for nestmates to stop by for a snack.

Living honeypots

Honeypot ants gather honeydew from insects or from plants. Inside their nests, these ants have living food stores. Certain worker ants are fed with honeydew until their bodies swell like balloons. They become living honeypots—so fat that they cannot walk! They hang from the roof of a chamber inside the ant nest.

When a nestmate is hungry, it goes to the storage chamber and taps a honeypot with its antennae. The honeypot brings up some honeydew from its stomach, which the hungry ant eats.

Bees Are Busy

There are thousands of kinds of bees. These useful insects produce honey and beeswax, but only the honey bees make enough for human use.

Bees depend on flowers for food. They collect grains of **pollen** (a powdery substance made by plants) and a sugary liquid called **nectar** from flowers. They make honey from the nectar. Bees eat honey and pollen.

How bees live

Most bees live alone, but some live in **colonies.** These bees are **social insects,** like ants. Inside each colony is a queen, along with tens of thousands of female worker bees, and a few hundred male bees, called drones.

Honey bees live in hives. The hive can be a wooden box or a hollow tree. Inside the hive, the bees build a honeycomb—a group of six-sided compartments called cells. Honeycombs are made of wax that the bees produce in their bodies.

A drone's life

A drone's only job is to mate with queens. Drones cannot feed from flowers, so they depend on workers to feed them. At the end of summer, when food becomes scarce, the workers stop feeding the drones. They drag them out of the hive to die.

When a colony becomes overcrowded, many of the workers and the old queen leave the hive as a swarm. The swarm clusters around a branch or a post after leaving the hive. Workers called scouts then seek out a location for the new colony.

Types of Bees

Worker   Queen   Drone

Solitary bees

Most kinds of bees live alone. But sometimes thousands of these solitary bees gather in a small area and build their nests close together. There are no worker bees among the solitary bees. Each female is like a queen who does her own work. Carpenter bees and mason bees are solitary bees.

Bee Facts

- A queen bee can lay a million eggs during her five-year lifetime.
- A bee colony may contain as many as 80,000 bees.
- A worker bee has a hard life. In summer, many worker bees die exhausted after six weeks.
- Honey bees can see colors and patterns. They can even see light rays invisible to the human eye!
- It isn't true that all bees sting. Some bite.

Each cell in a honey bee hive has six sides. The bees suck up nectar from flowers with their long tongues and store the nectar in their honey stomachs. Back at the hive, they spit up the nectar back through their mouth and put nectar in each cell. As the water in the nectar dries, the nectar changes into honey. The bees seal the cells with wax caps.

Meet the Beetles

Beetles make up the largest group of insects. They live everywhere. Beetles are found in rain forests and deserts, in cold places, and in hot places. Some can even survive in city sewers.

Beetles have a pair of front wings that are unlike the wings of any other insects. A beetle's wings form a leathery cover that acts like armor to protect the insect's body. Scientists named the beetles Coleoptera, which is Greek for "sheath wings."

Not so tough

Some beetles look fierce with their big horns and jaws. A few of these insects can bite if you disturb them. But most beetles hide or fly away when in danger.

The harlequin beetle lives in tropical forests in Mexico and South America. Its long legs help the animal to climb the trees on which it feeds.

The giraffe weevil lives in the forests of Madagascar. It gets its name from the long neck of the males. They use their long necks to compete for mates.

The ladybug is a small, round beetle known for its bright colors and spots. Ladybugs are often bright red or yellow, with black, red, white, or yellow spots.

The eyed click beetle is named for the spots behind its head. These big "eyes" might scare off a hungry bird.

Beetle Facts

- Many kinds of beetles play dead to fool a hungry bird or lizard.

- Water beetles can eat snails, tadpoles, and even small fish.

- Deathwatch beetles knock their heads against the wood in which they live. People used to think that the ticking sound foretold a death in the house. The American drugstore beetle is also known as the deathwatch beetle.

True Bugs

Many people call all insects bugs. But true bugs are insects belonging to the group called Hemiptera.

Bug features

Some bugs have wings, but others do not. Unlike other insects, bugs have no chewing mouthparts, but they do have horny snouts that look like beaks. They suck blood from animals or juices from plants.

Bugs in bed

You would not want bed bugs sleeping with you! These bugs are pests that bite people and animals and then suck their blood. Bed bugs probably don't spread disease, but their bite causes the skin of some people to swell and itch.

Bed bugs are small, wingless insects that feed on blood. The tiny insects are only 1/4 inch (6 millimeters) long when full-grown.

Water striders have long, stiltlike back legs that enable them to dart across the water's surface. They do not actually swim.

The harlequin bug is a stink bug native to Mexico and Central America. It has invaded parts of North America, damaging food crops.

The backswimmer swims upside down. It can stay underwater for hours. When hungry, the bug swims up beneath an insect on the surface and grabs it. ▼

Bugs in water

Some bugs live in water. Among these insects are water striders, backswimmers, and water boatmen. The water boatman has long, flat back legs that are covered with hairs. The bug uses these legs like oars when it swims.

Pew!

Stink bugs give off an unpleasant smell when they are disturbed. The stink bug's body is shaped like a shield.

Flies Are Fast

Flies are among the fastest of all flying insects. There are thousands of different kinds of flies. They include the common house fly, black flies, deer flies, fruit flies, gnats, horse flies, and mosquitoes, among others.

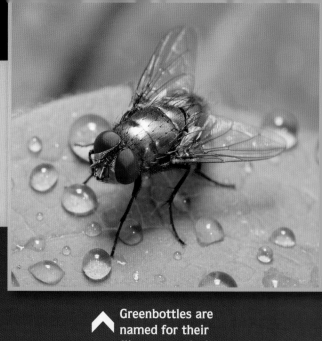

▲ Greenbottles are named for their metallic green coloring.

Two wings

All true flies have two wings. Some other insects are called flies—such as butterflies and dragonflies. But these insects have four wings. They are not true flies.

Fancy fliers

Flies fly in a remarkable way. They do not need to run or jump to get into the air. As soon as a fly beats its wings, it is flying. The wings keep on beating until the fly's feet touch something on which it can land.

Flies have no back wings. Instead, they have rodlike parts called halteres *(HAL tuhrs)* that vibrate in time with the beat of the fly's wings. The halteres balance the insect as it flies and help it dart quickly in any direction.

What a fly sees

A fly has large eyes, which helps it to look out for danger and for food. A house fly has about 4,000 lenses in each eye. Each lens gives the insect a slightly different picture. Everything a fly sees seems to be broken up into small bits. A fly does not see images clearly, but its eyes catch even the slightest movement.

Mosquitoes lay their eggs in or near water. Only female mosquitoes bite, and only a few kinds attack people and animals to sip their blood.

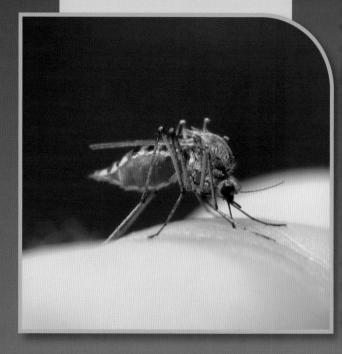

The house fly's life cycle

Like nearly all other insects, flies lay eggs. House flies lay their eggs in dung or food waste. Each egg hatches into a wriggling **larva,** called a maggot. The maggot eats and grows and then becomes a **pupa.** The adult fly forms inside the pupa.

Disease carriers

Some flies are among the most dangerous pests known. They carry germs inside their bodies, on the tip of their mouthparts, or in the hair on their bodies. When a fly "bites," or when it touches any object, it may leave some of these germs behind. Flies carry germs that cause serious diseases in people and other animals. Flies also cause diseases that affect plants.

Not all flies are pests. Some kinds of flies are helpful. They carry **pollen** from one plant to another. Other flies eat harmful insects. Scientists use fruit flies in the study of heredity. These flies provide valuable information on how characteristics are passed on from one generation to the next.

How Long Does a House Fly Live?

A house fly lives about 21 days in summer and longer in cool weather when flies are less active.

What Happens to Flies in Winter?

Most adult flies die in winter. Some hibernate. Many larvae and pupae live through the winter and develop into adults in the spring.

Fly Facts

- The buzzing of a fly is the sound of its wings beating.
- A house fly beats its wings about 200 times a second.
- A mosquito's wings beat about 1,000 times a second.

Life Cycle of a Fly

| Eggs | Maggots | Pupa | Adult Fly |

Beautiful Butterflies

Many people think that butterflies are the most beautiful of all insects. Butterflies come in every color imaginable. They flutter from flower to flower in summer. Their beauty and grace have inspired many artists and poets.

Butterflies and moths belong to the same group of insects—Lepidoptera *(LEHP uh DOP tuhr uh)*. The name comes from two Greek words meaning "scale wing." Powdery scales cover the wings of both butterflies and moths. Many moths are just as pretty as butterflies, but they fly at night, so people do not often see them.

Brilliant colors

The scales on a butterfly's wings overlap. Most scales contain pigment (coloring matter). They produce black, brown, red, white, and yellow colors. Other kinds of scales reflect light, much the way soap bubbles do. These scales produce shiny greens and blues.

The Queen Alexandra's birdwing is native to Papua New Guinea. It is the world's biggest butterfly, with wings about 11 inches (28 centimeters) across.

The tiger swallowtail lives in North America. Swallowtails are large butterflies with long tips that extend to their back wings. These tips look like the tails of certain birds called swallows.

Butterfly Facts

- The ancient Greeks believed that a person's soul left the body after death in the form of a butterfly.

- A butterfly cannot fly if it is too cold. It "warms up" by sunning itself or shivering its wings until its flight muscles have absorbed enough heat.

- Butterflies have weak legs and cannot walk far.

- A butterfly caterpillar may eat many times its own weight in food in one day.

The common Australian crow is a member of the milkweed family of large, slow-flying butterflies.

How to Tell a Butterfly from a Moth

- Most butterflies fly in the daytime. Most moths fly at night.

- Most butterflies have knobs at the ends of their **antennae**. Most moths do not.

- Most butterflies have slender, hairless bodies. Most moths have plump, furry bodies.

- Most butterflies rest with their wings held upright. Most moths rest with their wings spread out flat.

Caterpillars Become Butterflies

There are thousands of **species** of butterflies. All of them start life as an egg, which hatches into a caterpillar. Caterpillars spend most of their time eating. They do so to store enough energy so they can transform into butterflies.

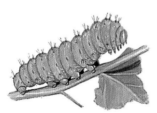

The postman butterfly ranges from Mexico to northern South America. The butterfly's markings warn that it is poisonous to other animals.

There are tens of thousands of kinds of moths, and they live all over the world. Moths have even been found on icecaps in the Arctic. Most moths fly at night.

Many moths are dull-colored. You do not notice them, especially when they are not moving. Some moths have bright spots or bands on their back wings, and a few are as colorful as butterflies.

What moths eat

Both moths and butterflies feed mainly on liquids, such as **nectar** from flowers. They suck up food through their **proboscis** *(proh BOS ihs)*—a long, hollow tube.

Moth caterpillars usually eat leaves and other parts of plants. They may also eat wood, the **larvae** of other insects, and clothing and other materials made of wool.

Unlike most moths, the male oak eggar moth flies by day. Oak eggars are found throughout Europe.

Stunt Flyers

Many bats hunt moths at night. The bat sends out high-pitched cries. When these sounds hit a moth, their echoes guide the bat to the insect. Some kinds of moths have a special hearing organ that picks up the bat's sounds. As soon as the moth hears a bat, it tries to escape. Often it begins flying in a jerky way, like a plane doing tricks. This gives it a better chance of escaping the hungry bat.

Slug caterpillar moths can be sulfur-yellow with hairy bodies. They are found throughout much of tropical Central and South America.

The Madagascar moon moth is known for its brilliant yellow coloring and striking red eyespots. The male moth has a wingspread of up to 9 inches (about 23 centimeters).

How many legs?

Like all insects, the caterpillars of butterflies and moths have six legs. A caterpillar also has eight false legs in the middle of its body. Its back end contains another pair of false legs that have suckers. This arrangement of real and false legs helps the caterpillar to crawl and hang onto plants as it feeds.

Insects can see, hear, touch, taste, and feel. The senses of many insects are much keener than those of most other animals. Even though they cannot talk as we do, insects communicate with others of their own kind.

How insects hear

Insects communicate with one another in various ways. Many make and hear sounds, though most insects have no ears. They hear sounds by means of delicate hairs on their **antennae** or on other parts of their bodies. Some insects can hear sounds that are too high or low for human ears.

A few insects do have ears, but they are usually on the sides of their bodies.

The katydid makes sounds by rubbing a back leg against a vein in a wing, like a violin player drawing a bow across a string. Other kinds of insects rub their wings together to make sounds.

Sounds without voices

Insects have no voices. Many make sounds by rubbing body parts together. The noisiest insects are probably grasshoppers, crickets, and cicadas. Usually only the males "sing" to attract females. Other insects, such as mosquitoes, are attracted by the beating of a female's wings. Many insects use sounds to find a mate.

Touch and taste

Insects are highly sensitive to touch. An insect's touch organs are the hairs and spines all over its body—even on its eyes. The gentlest air current moves these hairs, alerting the insect to changes in its environment.

Some insects have an amazingly sharp sense of taste. They taste things to find out if they are good to eat. Most insects have taste organs on their mouthparts. However, ants and wasps taste by touching food with their antennae. Honey bees and some butterflies taste with their feet. If they step on something tasty, they stop to eat it.

Smelling a friend

Many insects use their sense of smell to find their way around and to find food. They smell things with their antennae. Ants and bees use their antennae to find out whether another ant or bee is part of their **colony.**

A Bug that Glows

The firefly, or lightning bug, is a beetle that can produce glowing or flashing light. Males flash a signal to attract females. Females flash back to show they are willing to mate. Special organs on the underside of a firefly's **abdomen** produce a chemical reaction to make the light.

Sometimes a hungry firefly of a different **species** flashes in answer to a male's signal. The male flies to meet her—and she eats him!

◀ Bees dance to show other bees where food is to be found. When a worker bee returns to the hive, it dances up the honeycomb in a figure-eight pattern. The faster it dances, the closer the food is. The direction of the bee's dance shows other bees which way to fly, using the sun as a guide.

Most insects have short lives. They quickly become adults, reproduce, and die. Their eggs hatch and grow into new adults in a few weeks. Many insects produce several generations in a season.

An ichneumon wasp drills its egg-laying organ into a tree, seeking the grubs of other insects. The wasp's young feed on these grubs, killing them. The young then form pupae and develop into adult wasps.

Most insects lay eggs, but some, such as certain **species** of cockroaches, flies, and beetles, give birth to live young. As a rule, insects do not take care of their young. After the male and female mate, the female lays the eggs and leaves them. When the eggs hatch, the young insects must take care of themselves.

Good parents

Earwigs are one of the few insects that care for their young. Earwigs keep their eggs clean, guard them until the young hatch, and then watch over the young. A few kinds of beetles also stay with their young after they are born, guarding and feeding them.

Metamorphosis

Only a small number of insects, such as silverfish, look like miniature versions of their parents when they hatch. A dragonfly comes out of its egg as a **nymph**—a water creature with no wings. A butterfly comes out of its egg as a caterpillar. It has to go through another stage, as a **pupa,** before it can become an adult. This change of form is called metamorphosis.

Most insects abandon their eggs, but earwigs guard them. When the eggs hatch, earwigs care for their young.

From egg to butterfly

When a female butterfly is ready to lay eggs, she finds a plant that her young will be able to eat when they hatch. She sticks the eggs onto the plant with a sticky substance made from her body. When the caterpillars hatch from the eggs, they eat their own eggshell and then start eating the plant leaves.

After a caterpillar reaches full size, it is ready to become a pupa—a temporary form in which the adult structures of the butterfly develop. A hard shell forms around the animal's body during this stage. Inside the shell, an amazing transformation takes place. When the shell splits open, out comes an adult butterfly. In an hour or so the butterfly is ready to fly away. It finds a mate, and the cycle starts all over again.

Did You Know?

In some species of insects, males are extremely rare. Female aphids can reproduce without the aid of a male at all. A queen honey bee needs just one mating period. After that, she can lay hundreds of eggs a day for the rest of her life. She is the mother of all the thousands of bees in the hive.

A butterfly goes through several stages of growth before becoming an adult.

Eggs

Caterpillar

Adult

Pupa

A dragonfly emerges from its nymph skin to become an adult insect. As a nymph, it sheds its skin several times.

Feeding

Insects can eat all kinds of food. Many eat plants. Some eat other insects. Insects eat fabrics, cork, paste, and even face powder! Because it is so small, an individual insect does not need much food.

Hungry caterpillars

Caterpillars hardly ever stop eating. They gobble away at plants until they reach full size. When a caterpillar becomes a butterfly, it eats different foods.

A butterfly has no chewing mouthparts for eating leaves. It uses its tubelike **proboscis** to suck up **nectar** from flowers. Most butterflies feed only on nectar. Some butterflies do not feed at all.

Crop munchers

Insects that feed on plants can harm the plants they eat. At times, thousands or even millions of insects arrive in one place at the same time. A swarm of locusts can destroy entire fields of crops.

Caterpillars feed on the leaves of a cabbage plant. Many kinds of caterpillars can damage food crops.

Many dung beetles shape animal waste into a ball. The beetles roll the ball away to be buried in the ground. There, it will provide food for the beetles' young. ➤

Hunters

Many insects are hunters that **prey** on other insects. Army ants travel in huge numbers. The army surrounds and attacks any insect it finds. Army ants can even consume such animals as mice and lizards.

Food gatherers

Ants and bees collect food and take it back to their nests. A few other insects also collect food. Dung beetles roll balls of animal dung to their **burrows.** The female beetle lays her eggs in the dung, which provides food for the young beetles after they hatch.

▲ Army ants are fierce insects with powerful jaws. They work together to catch insects much larger than themselves.

Food Fit for a Queen

Baby bees are fed by "nurse" bees on royal jelly, a creamy food that is rich in vitamins and proteins. Worker bees produce the food in their bodies. After three days, the nurse bees switch to feeding the babies on bee bread, a mixture of honey and **pollen.** Sometimes a few chosen babies are fed only on royal jelly. These babies grow up to be queens.

Insect Homes

Most insects have no homes. But a few kinds of insects live in large groups called colonies. They build homes with many rooms and connecting passages.

Tent caterpillars spin white, tentlike webs in trees. These webs serve as nests for the caterpillars.

Diggers, carpenters, and weavers

Ants are called **social insects** because they live in **colonies.** Many ants share a nest. Ants build different types of nests. Most make their homes underground, carving out chambers and tunnels in the soil. Some build mounds of soil, twigs, and pine needles over their nests. Inside are tunnels that lead to nurseries for young ants, as well as storerooms and special rooms for use in cold or rainy weather.

Carpenter ants chew tunnels in wood. Tropical weaver ants make nests from tree leaves. To make a nest, some workers hold the edges of the leaves together, while others carry silk-spinning ant **larvae** back and forth across the edges. The larvae make a sheet of silken webbing that binds the leaves together.

Bees and wasps

Bees and wasps are also talented nest-builders. Honey bees make wax hives with many cells. Some cells serve as nurseries for young bees. Others are used to store food.

Some wasps build nests with many cells out of paper. Others dig nesting **burrows** in the ground. Still others take over burrows abandoned by beetles. They make separate rooms for each young wasp using bits of grass, stone, or mud. Daubers and potter wasps make nests out of mud.

Hornets are wasps that build large paper nests out of chewed-up wood and plant material.

Mound builders

Termites are insects that thrive in warm climates. Some termites mix soil with saliva to make a kind of cement. They build huge mound-nests. These nests may be as high as three adults standing on one another's shoulders!

Termites avoid sunlight and build underground tunnels to find food. Inside the termite mound, there are numerous chambers and galleries. The termite king and queen live in the center of the nest.

Some kinds of soil-dwelling termites build nests up to 20 feet (6 meters) tall. These complex mounds have thick outer walls and numerous inner chambers and tunnels.

Tropical weaver ants construct nests from tree leaves. They use silk from larvae as glue to bind the edges of the leaves together.

Going Places

Insects can walk, climb, and fly. Some insects swim. Others dig underground tunnels. Insects move about to find food and mates or to escape danger.

How insects walk

The middle section of an insect's body, called the **thorax,** has three segments, or parts. One pair of legs is connected to each segment. Each leg has five main segments, with movable joints or "knees" between them.

Steady on their feet

When humans walk, we balance ourselves on one leg as we step forward with the other. When insects walk, they usually move the middle leg on one side along with the front and hind legs on the other side. The insect always has three legs on the ground to support its body and keep it steady.

Swimmers

Some insects are built for life in the water. Backswimmers have long hind legs, which they use like a pair of oars. Water scorpions have a snorkellike device that they push up through the water to get air.

Diggers

Mole crickets and dung beetles use their broad front legs like shovels for digging in the soil. Nut weevils have a long, slender beak—often as long as the rest of their bodies—which they use to bore into nuts.

Grasshoppers and crickets use their long hind legs for jumping.

Some caterpillars move in very odd ways. The measuring worm caterpillar crawls by arching its body in loops.

Dragonflies have four large wings. They can fly faster than any other insect. They reach speeds of about 38 miles (61 kilometers) an hour.

Did You Know?

Flies have claws on their feet that help them cling to walls and ceilings. House flies also have hairy pads on their feet. A sticky substance on the feet helps the insects walk on smooth, slippery windows or on ceilings.

Jumpers and carriers

Locusts, fleas, and grasshoppers use their long, muscular hind legs for jumping. A grasshopper can leap about 20 times as far as the length of its body!

Worker bees have special "baskets" on their hind legs for carrying **pollen.** The outside of each of the hind legs is surrounded by long, curved hairs. Hairs on the inside of the hind legs help load pollen into the pollen basket. When the worker returns to the hive, it places its hind legs down into a cell and kicks off the pollen. Another worker uses its head to flatten out the pollen on the bottom of the cell.

Flying

Flying insects use two sets of muscles to beat their wings. One set makes the wings move up. The other set makes the wings move down. Other muscles at the base of the wings control the direction of flight. Many insects can hover like a helicopter or even fly backward.

Some Unusual Legs and Feet

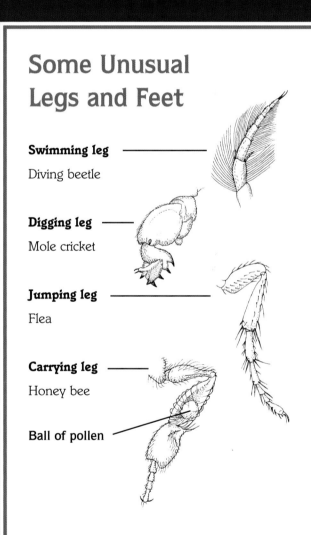

Swimming leg
Diving beetle

Digging leg
Mole cricket

Jumping leg
Flea

Carrying leg
Honey bee

Ball of pollen

Dealing With Danger

How do insects escape the many animals that hunt them? Some insects have weapons to defend themselves. Others have developed tricks to help them make a quick getaway.

Most insects can sense a **predator** in time to run or fly away. If you try to swat a fly, it usually takes off before your hand gets close. Tiny hairs on the fly's body detect movements in the air made by your hand.

Insect weapons

Bombardier (*BOM buh DIHR*) beetles and earwigs are among the insects that use a harmful spray against predators. Stinkbugs, lacewings, and carrion beetles give off a foul smell. Some ants, stag beetles, and other insects bite attackers with their jaws. Bees, wasps, and some ants have poisonous stings. And other insects, including some butterflies and moths, taste so bad that other animals leave them alone.

The bombardier beetle defends itself by squirting a spray. The spray is hot and irritating. The beetle has two organs at the end of its body that mix chemicals to make the spray. Earwigs, roaches, and many other insects also use chemical weapons.

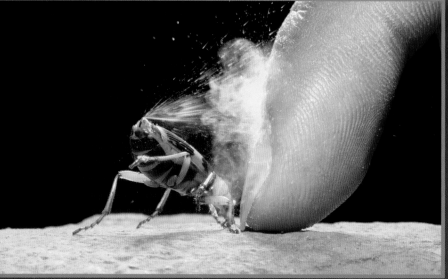

The saddleback caterpillar looks like a walking cactus. Any animal that gets too close is pricked by the spiky hairs. The hairs break when they pierce the animal's skin, releasing a poison.

A Bee's Stinger

The object in the picture below may look like a spear, but it's really a magnified photograph of a honey bee's stinger. The stinger grows from the end of the worker bee's body. It has barbs (hooks) on it. When the bee stings an attacker, the barbs hold tight and the stinger is pulled out of the bee's body. Muscles inside the stinger push it deeper into the attacker, releasing poison into the wound.

Worker bees can sting only once. They usually die soon afterward. Queen bees have smooth, curved stingers. They sting only to kill other queens, and they do not lose their stingers like worker bees.

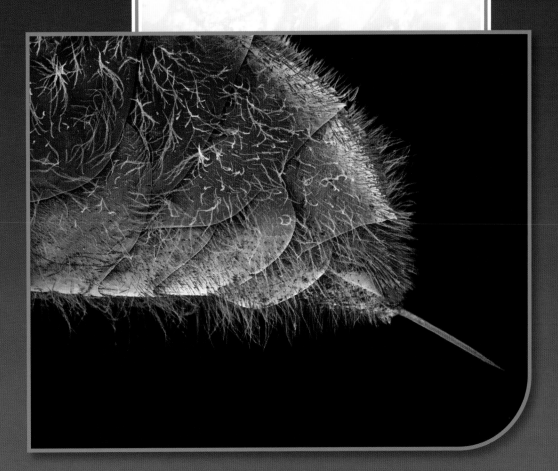

Hide and Seek

Many insects are hard to see. Some look like sticks, green leaves, dry leaves, or snail shells. Others look like thorns, dry reeds, or bird droppings. Some are so well disguised that you need to get really close to see them at all. They play hide and seek to fool hunting animals.

Protective coloration

Many insects have some form of camouflage *(KAM uh FLAHZH)*, or a means of blending into their natural background. For example, green insects often live on green plants. Brown insects may spend most on their time on the forest floor or on the branches of trees. When they rest on tree trunks, many brown spotted moths look like bark or bird droppings. This form of camouflage is called protective coloration.

Can you see the treehopper on the stem of this rosebush? It looks so much like a thorn that birds often overlook the insect.

Which is the twig and which is the insect? The walkingstick's long, thin body and sticklike legs make it very hard to see.

Living twigs

Walkingsticks are brown or green insects that look like twigs. Even when they move, it is hard to spot them. Some caterpillars look like twigs, too. Tree-hoppers look like the thorns and spines of plants. Insects that look like twigs or leaves have a good chance of escaping the notice of a **predator.**

Beware this leaf!

Disguise can also aid an insect looking for its next meal. Some praying mantises have long bodies and broad, leaflike wings. They look like torn leaves when they stand still. If another insect comes too close, a praying mantis will grab it.

A moth rests on tree bark. When it keeps still, the moth's coloring helps it to blend perfectly with the bark on the tree. The same moth resting on a flower or green grass would be seen much more easily.

The wings of the Indian leaf butterfly look like dead leaves. This helps the animal to hide from predators in its forest habitat.

Look-Alikes

Some insects mimic, or look like, another kind of insect. Why should this be? A harmless insect may mimic an insect that has weapons. Many dangerous insects also look alike, so other animals know to stay away from them all.

Keep off!

You may notice a wasp as soon as it lands near you. Most bees and wasps have black and yellow stripes to warn **predators** of their stingers. A bird or lizard that has an unpleasant encounter with one bee or wasp will know to avoid all the others.

Some kinds of harmless insects mimic insects that are poisonous or have weapons. Robber flies look so much like bumble bees that other animals avoid them, even though the flies have no sting. Some kinds of beetles, hoverflies, and drone flies also look like bees or wasps.

The robber fly looks like a bee, but it does not have the stinger of a bee.

The antlike spider is a spider that mimics an ant. Its body shape is more like an ant's than a spider's.

The markings of a tiger swallowtail caterpillar give the animal the appearance of a snake. When threatened, the caterpillar can even produce a snake's "tongue" by pushing out a small, pink organ.

Look-alike killers

Being a look-alike can also help a hunter. Assassin bugs mimic the kind of insect that they hunt. One kind of assassin bug looks just like a walkingstick. Another could pass for a mosquito. There is even an assassin bug that looks like a praying mantis. This mimicry helps the assassin bug come close to its **prey** without being recognized.

An ant or not?

Take a close look at the "ant" that appears on page 38. It has an ant's body, but count the legs. This animal has eight legs. It is not an ant. It is not even an insect. It is an antlike spider—a spider that deceives its prey by looking like an ant!

Mimicry can also involve behavior. Some kinds of assassin bugs pluck on the threads of a spider's web. They mimic the struggles of an insect caught in the web. When the spider arrives to collect its meal, the assassin bug eats it instead.

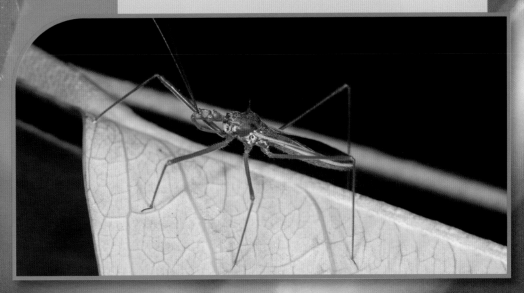

Insects and Flowers

Insects need flowers, but flowers also need insects. Many insects depend on flowers for food, and many flowers rely on insects to reproduce. Insects carry the yellow pollen that fertilizes the female parts of flowers. That enables the flowers to produce seeds.

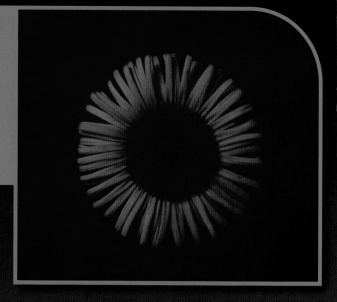

Bees, butterflies, and some beetles and flies feed on **nectar.** They find this sugary liquid in flowers. When an insect lands on a flower in search of food, **pollen** grains from the flower stick to its body.

When the insect visits other flowers, some of these pollen grains brush off onto these flowers. In this way, flowers of the same kind exchange pollen and are able to make seeds to reproduce. Apples, plums, oranges, and grapes are among the thousands of plants that use insects for **pollination.**

Attracting insects

Most flowers that are pollinated by insects are brightly colored or heavily scented. Different insects are attracted by different colors and scents. Many insects pollinate only certain kinds of flowers. For example, some kinds of bumble bees pollinate only such deep-chambered flowers as red clover.

Bees are strongly attracted to yellow, violet, and blue flowers. Unlike people, bees can see **ultraviolet** light. Many flowers, particularly yellow ones, have ultraviolet markings, and these markings attract bees.

The picture on the bottom shows how we see yellow flowers. When photographed in ultraviolet light (top), the same flower appears as a bee sees it. The dark areas are target zones, where the insect will find nectar and pollen.

Night scents

Many flowers that attract moths open only at night, when many moths search for food. These flowers are usually pale or white, so they are easier to see in the darkness. They also give off heavy scents that attract moths and other night-flying insects.

Beetles also pollinate flowers. They feed on white or pale flowers with spicy scents, such as magnolias or wild roses.

Flies do not have the long sucking mouthparts needed to drink nectar from deep-chambered flowers. For this reason, they like such flat flowers as buttercups. Flies are also drawn to certain flowers that give off a foul smell similar to rotting food.

Collecting pollen

The structure of many flowers ensures that visiting insects bring pollen from other flowers and take away new pollen. For example, to reach the nectar in a snapdragon flower, a bee has to push its way inside. In doing so, it brushes off pollen dust it has picked up from other flowers. Then, as it scrambles out, the bee is covered with a dusting of the flower's own pollen. It carries this pollen away to other flowers.

The Yucca Moth

The yucca flowers of the southwestern United States are pollinated only by the yucca moth. The female moth carries pollen from one yucca plant to a flower on a second yucca plant. The moth lays its eggs in the second flower and then deposits pollen from the first flower onto the seed-making parts of the second flower. The moth eggs and the yucca seeds develop together. The eggs hatch into caterpillars, which feed on the seeds. Enough seeds remain to grow into new yucca plants.

A bee's hairy body becomes covered with pollen as it moves from flower to flower.

Mass Movements

Some insects travel in large numbers and across long distances. These mass movements are called migrations. Despite their small size, some insects fly over mountain ranges and other barriers during their migrations.

Butterflies on the move

Every fall, North American monarch butterflies gather in great clouds. They fly south to spend the winter in warmer areas. Monarchs may travel up to 2,000 miles (3,200 kilometers) from Canada and the northern United States to a mountainous region in central Mexico. In the spring, the butterflies drift northward again, laying eggs as they go. Few monarchs live long enough to complete the return trip. Their young, after becoming adults, continue the northward journey.

Other butterflies that migrate include the painted lady and the red admiral, which fly between Europe and North Africa.

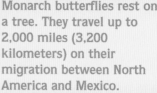

Monarch butterflies rest on a tree. They travel up to 2,000 miles (3,200 kilometers) on their migration between North America and Mexico.

Locusts by the million

Many other insects make long migratory flights. The locusts are probably the best known. Locusts often travel in swarms (large groups) so huge that they block out the sun.

Scientists do not know why locusts migrate. These insects live in hot countries, so they do not need to fly to warmer areas for the winter. And they do not migrate because they are hungry, either. In fact, locusts may leave a land where food is plentiful and not stop to feed during most of their long flight. The signal for the mass flight seems to be the build-up of an enormous population. A swarm of migrating locusts may number in the billions. Wherever they settle, they devastate plant life.

Hibernation

Many insects die when winter approaches, but others live through the cold by entering into a sleeplike state called hibernation. Some insects hibernate in the egg or **larval** stage. Others hibernate as adults. They spend the winter in barns, cellars, attics, caves, holes in trees, **burrows** in the ground, or other places that are sheltered from the winter weather. You may even find insects hibernating in your house. Insects that can survive the winter include house flies, mosquitoes, ladybugs, and some moths and butterflies.

Why bees swarm

Bees swarm when their **colony** becomes overcrowded. The queen bee lays eggs from which new queens will hatch before she and many of the worker bees leave the nest. Some workers stay behind to care for the new queen, who must first kill her rivals. The swarming bees fly away and cling together in a large mass, while scouts look for a site to start a new nest.

A swarm of bees hangs from a tree. Thousands of bees cluster together while scout bees search for a site for a new hive.

◀ Migrating brown locusts hover above the ground in South Africa. A locust swarm may devour food crops and leave farms in ruin.

All insects have their place in the great web of life. But some insects are considered pests because they damage crops, food, and houses. Others may carry deadly diseases.

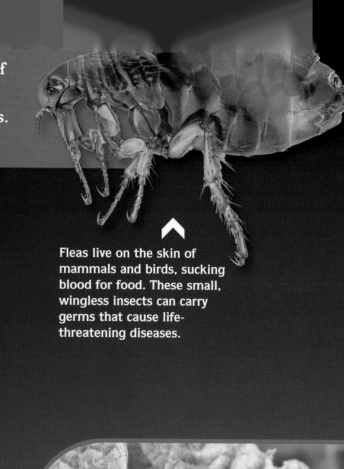

Fleas live on the skin of mammals and birds, sucking blood for food. These small, wingless insects can carry germs that cause life-threatening diseases.

Only a small number of insects are harmful. However, some insects eat valuable crops. Such pests include the boll weevil, which damages cotton plants; the Hessian fly, which attacks wheat; and the Colorado beetle, which feeds on potato plants.

Household pests

Many insects are household pests. Clothes moths eat clothing, and carpet beetles damage carpets and upholstery. Silverfish damage books, and termites chew through furniture and wood in buildings. Cock-roaches eat or spoil food in homes, restaurants, and warehouses.

Disease carriers

Some bloodsucking insects carry diseases. Mosquitoes may carry deadly malaria. A kind of biting fly carries sleeping sickness.

Colorado potato beetles lay their eggs on potato plants. Both the adult beetles and the **larvae** feed on the leaves of the plants.

eats the leaves and fruits of about 275 kinds of plants! Its **larvae** eat the roots.

The European bark beetle is one of two kinds of bark beetles that spread Dutch elm fungus disease. The disease kills elm trees.

Don't Let the Bed Bugs Bite!

Bed bugs are small, wingless insects that feed on blood. They like to live near the sleeping quarters of their victims—or even in their beds. Their small size and flattened bodies make it easy for them hide in tiny cracks or between floorboards.

Bed bugs disappeared from North America for 40 years, but they made a comeback beginning in the late 1990's. They have since infested hotels, homes, theaters, clothing stores, and offices in cities throughout the world. Scientists are not sure why their populations have exploded so fast, but travel is believed to have helped them spread.

Bed bugs probably don't spread disease, but their bite can irritate the skin of some people. And it can be extremely difficult—and expensive—to get rid of them. For now, just about the only ones benefiting from this **parasite's** comeback are the exterminator businesses that are hired to fight them.

Useful Insects

We think of some insects as useful and others as harmful. But all insects are useful in some way. They are an important part of the balance of nature. Without them, life as we know it would not exist.

Food for others

Insects are an important food source for birds, fish, frogs, lizards, and many small mammals. Insects are even consumed by a few meat-eating plants, such as the Venus's-flytrap, pitcher plants, and sundew plants.

Insect products

Insects provide us with many useful products. Honey and beeswax are made by bees. Silk moth caterpillars, known as silkworms, produce silk. Shellac, a varnish, comes from a sticky substance produced by a scale insect. Cochineal, a bright-red dye, comes from the dried bodies of the cochineal scale insect.

Farmers' friends

Farmers need insects because bees, wasps, flies, butterflies, and other insects **pollinate** plants. Many fruits depend on insects to spread their **pollen.** Without the insects' help, these plants would not make seeds. Peas, onions, carrots, cabbages, and clover also depend on insects for pollination. So do many garden flowers.

Beekeepers keep bees in hives. The bees build their honeycombs in drawerlike sections that can be taken out of the hive. Some beekeepers wear special clothing to protect their bodies from bee stings. A few experienced bee-keepers handle bees and honeycombs with their bare hands.

When silkworm caterpillars are ready to become **pupae**, they spin cocoons, or outer wrappings, of fine silk. Today, cultivated silk is spun by silkworms raised on silk farms.

Pitcher plants depend on insects for nutrients. They trap insects inside their pitcher-shaped leaves.

Waste removers

Many insects help keep the world clean. They are waste removers, feeding on animal wastes and the bodies of dead animals.

Pest controllers

Some insects eat harmful pests. The ladybug, for example, eats aphids. Other insects are **parasites** that live in or on the bodies of harmful insects. Some wasps lay their eggs on caterpillars that damage tomato plants. As the young wasps develop, they feed on the caterpillars and kill them.

Useful Insects **47**

Spiders

Spiders live in the same kinds of places as insects. Some people are afraid of spiders. Many others find them fascinating. Spiders are best known for the silk webs they spin. All spiders spin silk, but not all spiders make webs.

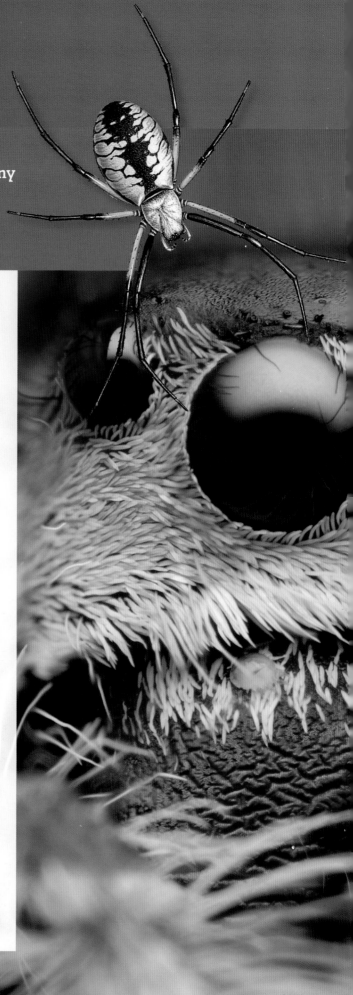

Arachnids

Spiders belong to the class of animals called arachnids. Arachnids are small, insectlike animals that have no wings. Ticks, mites, scorpions, and daddy longlegs are also arachnids.

All arachnids have four pairs of legs but have no **antennae.** Most have one to six pairs of simple eyes, but some **species** are eyeless.

Spider bodies

A spider's body has two main parts—the head and **abdomen.** A spider's eyes lie on top and near the front of its head. Most species have eight eyes, arranged in two rows of four each.

A spider's mouth opening lies below the eyes. Spiders do not have chewing mouthparts, and they swallow only liquids. Extensions around the mouth form a short "straw" through which the spider sucks the body fluid of its victim. Spiders also have a pair of mouthparts that the spider uses to seize, crush, and kill its **prey.**

Spider bites

All spiders have fangs, and all except a few have poison glands. Spiders use their fangs and poison glands to kill prey. A spider's bite can paralyze or kill insects and other small animals. Although spiders feed mostly on insects, larger spiders may occasionally capture and eat tadpoles, small frogs, fish, birds, or even mice.

Spider Facts

- Most spiders have eight eyes. Some spiders have six, four, or two eyes, and some have no eyes at all.
- A spider has no bones. Its body is covered in a tough skeleton, like a suit of armor.
- Spiders have fangs for biting prey, but they cannot chew their food. A spider softens the solid parts of its victims by spraying digestive juice on them. It then sucks up the liquid food through a mouthpart that works like a built-in straw.
- Some spiders can live for a year without eating.

Spiders everywhere

Spiders live anywhere they can find food. They can be found in fields, woods, swamps, caves, and deserts. They also live in houses. One kind of spider spends most of its life underwater. Another kind lives near the top of Mount Everest, the world's highest mountain.

The funnel-web spider is a poisonous Australian spider. It lives in **burrows,** for which it spins a funnel-shaped entrance.

Amazing Silk Spinners

Spider silk is the strongest natural fiber known. It is made by special glands in the spider's body. Some glands make a liquid silk that dries outside the body. Other glands make a silk that stays sticky.

Silk varieties

Spiders spin silk with short, fingerlike organs called **spinnerets.** Using different spinnerets, a spider can mix silk from different silk glands to make a very thin thread or a thick band of silk. Some spiders make beaded threads to help them trap jumping or flying insects. Others spin very thin threads of extremely sticky silk. The spider weaves sticky threads and dry threads into a ribbonlike thread called a hackled band. It uses this band to catch and tie up its **prey.**

Hanging by a thread

Spiders depend on silk in so many ways that they could not live without it. Most spiders drag a silk thread behind them everywhere they go. This thread, called a dragline, can help the spider escape from **predators.** If a hungry bird comes too close to its web, the spider can use its dragline to drop from the web to the ground or to hang in the air. When the danger has passed, the spider climbs back up the dragline to its web. Hunting spiders use their draglines to swing down to the ground from high places.

A spider's dragline is also called a "lifeline" because it can help the spider to escape from hunters.

Orb Weavers

Orb weavers build the most beautifully patterned webs of all. They weave their round webs in open areas, often between tree branches or flower stems. Threads of dry silk extend from an orb web's center like the spokes of a wheel. Coiling lines of sticky silk connect the spokes and serve as an insect trap.

An orb weaver typically spins a new web every night. The spider eats the old web. This way, it reuses the silk and eats any tiny insects it might have missed.

A spider spins silk with fingerlike spinnerets on the rear of its **abdomen**. Liquid silk made in the silk glands flows through the spinnerets to the outside, where it hardens into threads.

Skilled Hunters

All spiders hunt animals for food. They catch insects and other small animals. Many spiders trap their prey. Others run swiftly to catch their victims, and some even hunt underwater.

Hunting spiders typically creep up on their **prey** or lie in wait and pounce on it. Their strong mouthparts help them to overpower their victims.

Many spiders seem to locate prey using vibrations transmitted through the ground. Some hunters have large eyes and can see their prey from a distance.

Big leapers

Jumping spiders sneak up and pounce on their prey. These spiders have short legs, but they can jump more than 40 times the length of their bodies! Jumping spiders also have excellent vision.

Hunting with nets

The ogre-faced spider holds its web in its front legs. The web is about the size of a postage stamp. When it spots an insect, the spider stretches the web to several times normal size. Then it sweeps the net over its prey.

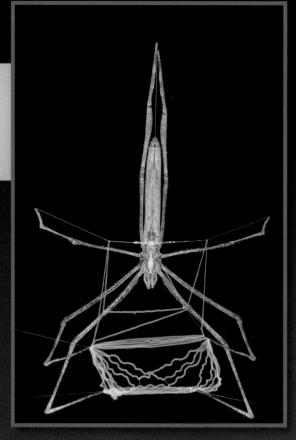

The ogre-faced spider spins a net that it casts at prey.

Jumping spiders can leap great distances to catch prey.

Spider giants

Tarantulas rank as the world's largest spiders. The biggest ones live in South American jungles. Great numbers of tarantulas also inhabit dry regions of Mexico and the southwestern United States.

Many tarantula **species** dig **burrows.** A California tarantula builds a small tower of grass and twigs at the entrance to its burrow. This spider then sits just below the rim and waits for insects to pass within striking distance.

Fishing for food

Nursery-web spiders, sometimes called fishing spiders, live near water and hunt insects, small fish, and tadpoles. These spiders have large bodies and long, thin legs. Because of their light weight, many can walk on water without sinking. They also can dive underwater for short periods. Many females in this group build special webs for their young.

Wolf spiders are excellent hunters. Many kinds have large, hairy bodies and run swiftly in search of food.

Some species of tarantula hunt large prey, like this colorful frog.

The Spider Life Cycle

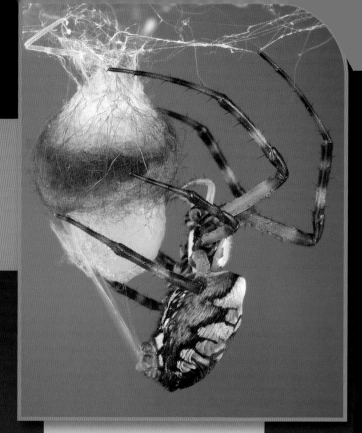

Most spiders live less than one year. But large species can live longer. Some female tarantulas have survived more than 20 years in captivity! Spiders become adults at different times of the year.

Spider courtship

Most spiders live alone. A male spider has to be very careful when he seeks a mate. Many males are much smaller than females, and females sometimes eat males. Many male spiders perform courtship displays. Some dance, waving the legs and body. Some shake the female spider's web. Some even offer the female a captured fly as a gift.

After laying her eggs, a female spider wraps them in an egg case to protect them.

Spider parents

Female spiders lay eggs. The number of eggs that a female spider lays at one time varies with her size. Females of many **species** lay about 100 eggs. But some of the smallest spiders lay just 1 egg, while some of the largest lay more than 2,000.

Most spiders enclose their eggs in a silken egg sac. In many species, the female spider dies soon after making the egg sac. But some mother spiders stay with the eggs or even carry them around. A few kinds of mother spiders keep the young in their web for a time. Mother and young share the captured insects.

A male jumping spider performs a courtship display for a nearby female.

Why Isn't a Spider Trapped by Its Own Web?

A web-spinning spider has a special hooked claw on each foot. When walking across the web, the spider grasps the silk lines with the hooks, so it never gets stuck.

How Does a Spider Know It Has Caught a Meal?

Most web-spinning spiders have poor eyesight. They respond to the movement of the web when an insect becomes caught. Some attach a special trap line to the web. The spider hides in its nest near the web, holding the line. When it feels a tug, the spider darts out to capture its **prey**.

A female wolf spider carries her spiderlings on her body, protecting them as they grow.

To leave home, spiderlings spin silk threads and balloon away on the wind.

Ballooning off

Baby spiders, called spiderlings, hatch inside the egg sac. When they are developed enough to leave, the spiderlings sometimes travel long distances from home. They climb to the top of a fence post or bush and tilt their **spinnerets** up into the air. The moving air pulls silk threads out of the spinnerets. The spider launches into the air like a balloon at the end of a string. This unusual way of leaving home is called ballooning.

Spiders have helped people for many thousands of years by eating harmful insects, including flies, mosquitoes, and such crop pests as aphids and grasshoppers. Spiders rank among the most important predators of these insects.

The brown recluse is a poisonous spider found in the United States. It is usually found outdoors under rocks, and indoors under furniture and in undisturbed areas.

Products made by spiders

Scientists believe spider silk and venom will prove useful to human beings. Spider silk, though extremely fine, has great strength and durability. Biologists study the microscopic structure of this silk to understand its unusual properties. They also study how spiders make the silk by using only a few kinds of proteins dissolved in water. These studies may help manufacturers develop new ways of producing extremely strong industrial fibers.

Spider venom can affect the human nervous system in many ways, and scientists have learned much about the nervous system by studying the effects of spider venom. Knowledge gained from these studies may lead to cures for illnesses of the nervous system, including Parkinson disease.

Manufacturers also hope to use spider venoms to make new kinds of insecticides—chemicals that kill insects. Collectively, the many different spider venoms may contain thousands of compounds that are highly poisonous to insects but harmless to people or other animals.

Artificial spider silk may provide manufacturers with an extremely strong and durable industrial fiber.

The redback spider is a poisonous spider common in Australia. People bitten by female redback spiders may become ill and suffer severe pain. However, deaths from redback bites have been nearly eliminated since the development of an antivenin (medicine used to combat animal venom) in the 1950's.

Dangerous spiders

Only a few kinds of spiders can inflict bites severe enough to endanger people. The most dangerous spider groups include the recluses and the widows of North America, the redbacks and funnel-web spiders of Australia, and the button spiders of Africa. The bites of these spiders can cause severe pain, but they rarely prove fatal. Moreover, spiders rarely bite people unless threatened.

Scorpions, mites, ticks, and daddy longlegs are animals related to spiders. They belong to the arachnid group.

Scorpions

Scorpions live in warm climates. Dozens of **species** live in the United States and Canada. A scorpion has eight legs, like a spider, but its body is a different shape. It has two tiny pincers near its head and two large claws. At the tip of the scorpion's slender tail is a poisonous sting. When hunting, the scorpion seizes its **prey** in its claws, and then curls its tail over its head to sting the prey to death. Scorpions eat insects and spiders. They are most active at night. Mother scorpions give birth to live young. The baby scorpions ride on their mother's back for several days.

A scorpion grabs prey with its powerful claws.

Ticks

Ticks are bigger than mites. When a tick egg hatches, a flat **larva** with six legs crawls out. It waits on a grass stalk or shrub until an animal passes by. Then the tick clings onto the animal, pierces the animal's skin with its beak, and feeds on its blood. The larva grows into an eight-legged **nymph,** and then into an adult tick, still hanging onto its host.

Some ticks cause diseases in human beings and domesticated animals. Deer ticks, also called black-legged ticks, transmit Lyme disease to human beings. If untreated, this disease can lead to chronic arthritis and heart and nerve disorders.

A deer tick becomes swollen with blood after it has eaten.

Mites

Some mites are too small to be seen without a microscope. Many kinds of mites are **parasites**—harmful pests that suck the blood of animals or the juices of plants. Other mites eat feathers, cheese, and flour. Mites **burrow** into the skins of such animals as horses, cattle, and poultry, and humans.

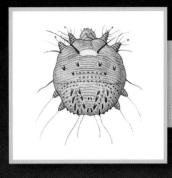

The itch mite has a baglike body.

Daddy longlegs

Daddy longlegs, also called harvestmen, are harmless, long-legged creatures that look similar to spiders. Daddy longlegs prey on small insects. They also eat dead insects and fallen fruit. When disturbed, many species of daddy longlegs can give off a bad odor, but they do not bite. Unlike spiders, daddy longlegs do not have fangs or spin webs.

In the tropics, some species gather in great enough numbers to cover a small bush. If disturbed, all the daddy longlegs will shake violently, causing the entire bush to move.

The pearleaf blister mite damages fruit trees.

Daddy longlegs are small animals related to spiders. They have eight long legs and an oval-shaped body,

The world of insects and spiders is full of amazing facts. Here are just a few.

Keen eyes. Some dragonflies have as many as 30,000 lenses in each eye.

Sweet tasters. Butterflies can taste the tiniest amounts of sugar in water. The amount of sugar detected by a monarch butterfly would have to be 2,000 times stronger before a person could taste it.

Fast fliers. The fastest-flying insects are probably dragonflies. They fly up to about 38 miles (61 kilometers) an hour.

Long-distance fliers. Butterflies and locusts can fly more than 100 miles (160 kilometers) without stopping to eat. They use food energy stored in their bodies. Tiny fruit flies can fly for more than five hours without needing to feed. A honey bee can fly for only 15 minutes before it needs to rest and refuel.

Changing skins. Insects and spiders shed their skins as they grow. A tarantula spider sheds its skin more than 20 times in its lifetime.

Goliaths. Wetas are large New Zealand insects that resemble grasshoppers. They may reach the size of a mouse, or about 4 inches (10 centimeters) in length. Despite their frightening appearance, wetas will not harm people if handled carefully, although the larger **species** can inflict a powerful bite.

Locusts ⏶

Tarantula ❯

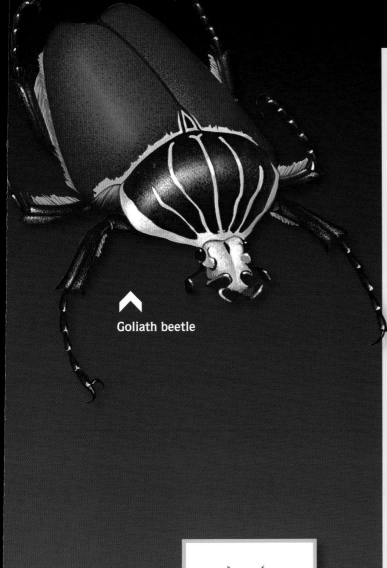

Goliath beetle

Fairy fly

Biggest crowd. A swarm of locusts seen near the Red Sea was so enormous that it was believed to cover an area five times the size of New York City! Locust swarms have been seen flying far out at sea, more than 1,000 miles (1,600 kilometers) from land.

The Goliath beetle is one of the largest and heaviest insects. It grows about 5 inches (13 centimeters) long and weighs over 1½ ounces (42 grams).

Mini-muscles. Large butterflies flutter their wings quite slowly—as few as four wingbeats a second. Some tiny midges beat their wings 1,000 times a second. The midges' wing muscles are probably the fastest-working muscles in the insect world!

The longest insects are probably walkingsticks. Some are more than 12 inches (30 centimeters) long.

Robbers and slavers. Thief ants live by stealing food from other ants. Many ants also raid other ants' nests and carry off the young, which they bring up in their own nest as slaves.

One of the smallest insects is the fairy fly. It can barely be seen by the unaided eye. The picture on this page shows a fairy fly greatly enlarged.

A queen termite may live as long as 50 years and is probably the longest-lived of all insects. She can lay eggs at a rate of 10,000 to 30,000 a day!

Glossary

abdomen the third and last section of the body of an insect.

antenna (plural: **antennae**) one of a pair of long feelers on the head of an insect.

burrow (n.) a hole dug in the ground by an animal for refuge or shelter; (v.) to dig a hole in the ground.

colony a group of animals of the same kind living together.

larva (plural: **larvae**) the early stage of life in some animals, when they may look quite unlike their parents.

nectar a sweet substance found in many flowers.

nymph any one of certain insects in the stage of development between egg and adult. It resembles the adult but lacks fully developed wings.

parasite a living thing that takes food or resources from another living thing.

pollen the yellow dust made by plants and found in flowers. This dust is made up of male cells. It is carried by the wind, insects, or birds, and fertilizes the female parts of flowers to form seeds.

pollinate; pollination to carry pollen from one flower to another; the act of carrying pollen from one flower to another.

predator a hunting animal.

prey (n.) any animal or animals hunted for food by another animal; (v.) to hunt or kill for food.

proboscis the tubelike mouthparts of some insects developed to great length for piercing or sucking.

pupa (plural: **pupae**) the stage in an insect's development between larva and adult.

social insect an insect that lives with other insects of its kind in colonies. Ants, honey bees, and termites are social insects.

species a group of living things with similar characteristics. Animals of the same species can breed with one another.

spinneret a spider's silk-making organ.

thorax the middle section of an insect's body.

ultraviolet rays of light invisible to people but not to some insects. Ultraviolet rays lie just beyond the violet end of the visible light spectrum.

Books

Bizarre Insects by Margaret Jean Anderson
(Enslow Publishers, 1996)

Centipedes, Millipedes, Scorpions and Spiders
by Daniel Gilpin (Compass Point Books, 2006)

Classifying Insects by Andrew Solway
(Heinemann Library, 2003)

Cockroaches, Cocoons, and Honeycombs
by Janice Parker (Raintree Steck-Vaughn, 2000)

**The Insecto-Files: Amazing Insect Science and
Bug Facts You'll Never Believe** by Helaine
Becker and Claudia Dávila (Maple Tree Press,
2009)

Killer Ants by Nicholas Nirgiotis and Emma
Stevenson (Holiday House, 2009)

**National Audubon Society First Field Guide:
Insects** by Christina Wilsdon (Scholastic, 1998)

Paleo Bugs: Survival of the Creepiest by Timothy
J. Bradley (Chronicle Books, 2008)

Spiderology by Michael Elsohn Ross and others
(Carolrhoda Books, 2000)

The Tarantula Scientist by Sy Montgomery and
Nic Bishop (Houghton Mifflin Co., 2004)

Websites

Amateur Entomologists' Society: Insects

http://www.amentsoc.org/insects/

The AES works to spread knowledge about the
insect world. This site contains fact sheets, tips
on conservation, and advice on becoming an
entomologist (person who studies insects).

Butterflies and Moths of North America

http://www.butterfliesandmoths.org/

The BAMONA project works to collect and
organize information about the many species of
butterflies and moths that populate North
America.

The Butterfly Lab

http://www.naturemuseum.org/online/thebutterfl
ylab/index.htm

Interactive diagrams on the anatomy, life cycles,
and behavior of butterflies, from the Peggy
Notebaert Nature Museum.

Entomology: BugInfo

http://www.si.edu/encyclopedia_SI/nmnh/buginfo/

Links provide information on dozens of different
insect-related topics, from pet insects to killer
bees.

Insects.org

http://www.insects.org

Profiles of different insects, complete with photo
galleries, are organized by their different orders
on this site.

Let's Talk About Insects

http://urbanext.illinois.edu/insects/

An animated guide to the insect world, from the
University of Illinois Extension program.

Natural History Museum: Insects and Spiders

http://www.nhm.ac.uk/nature-online/life/insects-
spiders/

Identify mystery bugs, join discussions in the
Bug Forums, and find out how bugs can help
solve crimes on this educational site.

Sci4Kids: Insects!

http://www.ars.usda.gov/is/kids/insects/insectintro
.htm

This educational site from the USDA Agricultural
Research Service provides informative stories
about different kinds of insects and their roles in
the world.

Index